Going to Mars

by Emily Wortman-Wunder

Table of Contents

Introduction 2

Chapter One
Earth's Neighbor 4

Chapter Two
The Rovers Solve a Problem 9

Chapter Three
The Rovers at Work 14

Chapter Four
The Future on Mars. 18

Conclusion. 21

Glossary 22

Index. 23

Comprehension Check. .24

Introduction

It is the evening of January 3, 2003. There are many scientists in the Jet Propulsion Laboratory in Pasadena California. They are all in the control room for the Mars Exploration Rovers project. This room is where scientists operate spacecrafts. One of two Mars **rovers**, *Spirit*, has entered the atmosphere of planet Mars and will soon land. The rover is traveling at about 12,000 miles an hour. Within the next six minutes, the rover needs to slow to zero miles per hour, so *Spirit* can land gently on Mars. A rover is a robot that is used to explore a planet.

Everyone in the room is waiting to see what will happen next. The last Mars **mission** ended in disaster because the Mars Polar **lander** did not land properly. More than 300 people have worked a long time to get *Spirit* to Mars. Everyone wants to learn what Spirit can tell us about the planet. Will it end in success or failure?

The lander carrying *Spirit* breaks ⊃ away from the rest of the spacecraft.

Chapter One

Earth's Neighbor

Mars is Earth's nearest neighbor. It has an environment that is similar to Earth in many ways. The <u>surface</u>, or outer layer, of Mars is much like the Earth's surface. It is dry and hard. Temperatures on Mars range from –225° to 60° Fahrenheit (-140° to 25° Celsius). Mars and Earth are different, too. The atmosphere, or the gases that surround a planet, of Mars is almost all carbon dioxide. There is not enough oxygen for humans to breathe. On Mars, there is less **gravity**, the force that pulls us toward the ground.

However, Mars is the planet in the **solar system** that seems most possible for humans to visit. Mars is close to Earth, and it has a surface and surface temperature that are most similar to Earth's.

Clue: You can learn what the word <u>surface</u> means by reading context clues, the words that come before and after it. Can you use context clues to find the meaning of the word *gravity* on this page?

4

Is There Life on Mars?

For many years, humans thought that Mars might have intelligent life, living creatures people call **Martians**. We worried that Martians might be dangerous.

We now know there is no intelligent life on Mars. But scientists think there may be **bacteria** on Mars, or that there used to be life similar to bacteria.

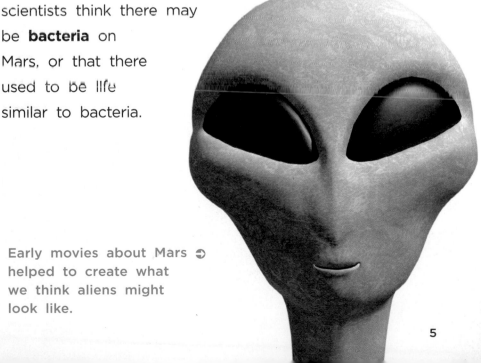

Early movies about Mars ⤴ helped to create what we think aliens might look like.

🎧 One of *Viking's* main goals was to look for signs of life.

Exploring Mars

Since the 1960s, people have used robots and **satellite** missions to explore Mars. The U.S. spacecraft *Mariner 4* took the first close-up photos of Mars in 1963. It did not land on Mars. Instead, it flew close to Mars to take pictures. Mars looked like a <u>barren</u> planet.

In 1976 the *Viking* **probes** landed on Mars and took soil samples. These were the first probes to land successfully on Mars. The *Viking* **orbiters**, spacecraft that circle the planet and never land, sent information about Mars. Scientists used the information to draw detailed maps of Mars's surface.

<u>barren:</u> unable to support life

Another orbiter, the *Mars Global Surveyor,* and the 1997 Pathfinder mission were the most recent successful missions to Mars. The Pathfinder mission landed a small rover on the surface of Mars. The rover's name was *Sojourner.* It functioned from July 4 to October 7, 1997. After *Sojourner* landed, scientists tried to land other rovers on Mars, but these attempts failed.

Different missions to Mars have mapped and photographed almost the entire planet from space, but we have not explored much of Mars's surface. *Sojourner* traveled an area that is smaller than an Olympic-size swimming pool. The two Viking probes stayed in one place while they took soil samples.

Pictures of Mars

We have learned much about the geography and geology of Mars from photographs. This photo shows the polar regions of Mars. Like Earth, the North and South poles of Mars are covered in ice.

We still have many unanswered questions about Mars. Did Mars once have rivers and lakes or water? If there was water, what happened to it? What do we need to make a space station on Mars where people can live and work? Scientists wanted to find answers to these questions when they <u>launched</u> the two Mars *Exploration* rovers in 2003.

<u>launch:</u> to send a spacecraft into space to begin its travel

↻ *Sojourner* took these photos. They show rocks and sand on Mars that look like they had been shaped and moved by water.

Chapter Two

The Rovers Solve a Problem

After several failed missions, Congress asked NASA (National Aeronautics and Space Administration) to keep costs low. NASA's project director Paul Theisinger had an idea for a new mission to Mars. It would only take three and a half years to launch, instead of the usual seven years. Scientists decided to use ideas and technology from earlier missions. So, the Mars *Exploration* rovers project would cost less money.

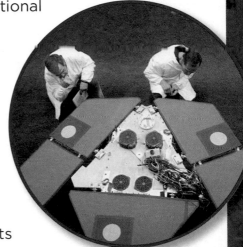

⌓ NASA scientists check equipment to make sure it is functioning properly.

Theisinger's idea was to send two <u>identical</u> rovers, *Spirit* and *Opportunity*, to opposite sides of Mars. Each rover had to be bigger to carry more instruments and they had to travel farther than any other missions to Mars.

<u>identical</u>: exactly the same

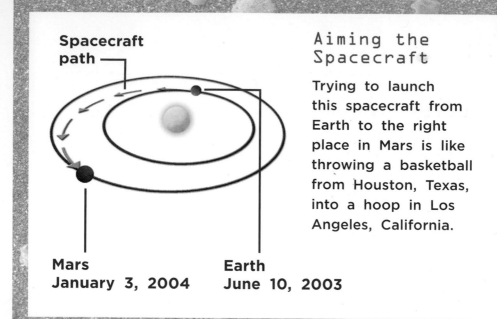

Spacecraft path

Aiming the Spacecraft

Trying to launch this spacecraft from Earth to the right place in Mars is like throwing a basketball from Houston, Texas, into a hoop in Los Angeles, California.

Mars
January 3, 2004

Earth
June 10, 2003

Getting Ready

Theisinger quickly gathered a team to work on the rover project. The engineering team adjusted the bigger, heavier rovers into the spacecraft model that worked for *Sojourner*. The scientists had to pick a spot on the surface of Mars to land the rovers. The **navigation** team had to make the rovers land on Mars on the right day and in exactly the right place. The team wanted to land the rovers on Mars in winter of 2004. During that winter Mars would be the closest to Earth than it had been in the past 60,000 years.

On the Way

In August 2002, scientists were ready to assemble Mars rovers *Spirit* and *Opportunity*. It was very important to make sure that *Spirit* and *Opportunity* did not carry any germs. NASA does not want to contaminate, or pollute, Mars with living materials from Earth. So, scientists wore masks, gloves, and body suits like doctors in an operating room.

Each rover was loaded into its lander. Then each lander was loaded onto a spacecraft. *Spirit* successfully launched on June 10, 2003. *Opportunity* successfully launched on July 7, 2003.

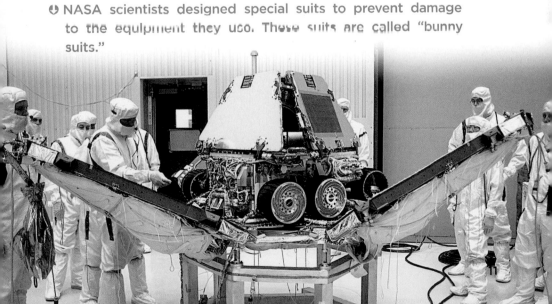

◔ NASA scientists designed special suits to prevent damage to the equipment they use. These suits are called "bunny suits."

11

While Mars rovers hurtled, or sped, toward Mars, the navigation team here on Earth constantly tracked the location of the rovers. Other scientists prepared for what would happen when the rovers landed.

It is very important that scientists know how to navigate the rovers when they are on Mars.

---

navigate: to safely guide or direct

Landing: The Hardest Part

1 **Just before the spacecraft enters the zone of Martian atmosphere, the lander separates from the cruise stage.**

2 **Five miles (8km) above the surface of Mars, parachutes open to slow the lander.**

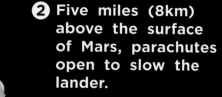

So, scientists at the Jet Propulsion Laboratory practiced with two model rovers that are similar to the rovers that were traveling to Mars. Every day, scientists practiced navigating the rovers through the rocky maze. The scientists told these rovers to collect soil samples, move over or around rocks, and take photographs.

3 Eight seconds before landing, the airbags inflate. Then the lander's rockets fire and cut the parachute away. The lander bounces across the surface of Mars.

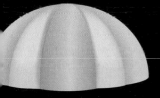

4 The airbags deflate, the lander opens, and the rover comes out.

Chapter Three

The Rovers at Work

On January 3, 2004, *Spirit* landed on Mars in the Gusev Crater. *Opportunity* landed on the opposite side of Mars about three weeks later.

Scientists built the rovers to last 90 Martian days, or **sols**, on the surface of Mars. During this time, the rovers traveled up to 40 meters a day and examined rocks, soil, and other landforms on Mars. Then they sent information back to Earth.

The rovers work during the daytime. However, daytime on Mars might be the middle of the night on Earth. NASA scientists had to work constantly to navigate the rovers and collect data, <u>so</u> they worked all day and night.

Clue: This is a compound sentence, two complete thoughts connected by <u>so</u>. Can you find a compound sentence on page 9? It is connected by the word *and*.

The Rover

The neck holds the camera head up at 1.4 meters (5 feet), or roughly the height of a human. It helps the camera see farther.

The rover has nine eyes, or cameras.

The antenna helps the rover talk and listen to scientists on Earth.

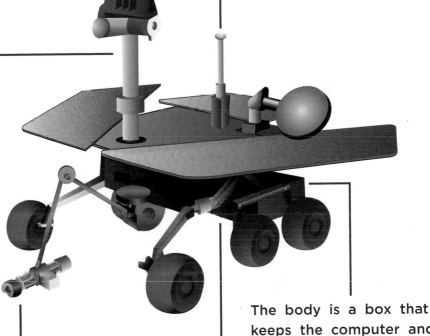

The body is a box that keeps the computer and other machines warm.

Inside the body is an onboard computer that works like a brain

The arm holds instruments that help the rover feel mars.

Spirit and *Opportunity* have discovered some important facts. The most exciting discovery came from *Opportunity* during its first day on Mars. It took a photo of an unusual rock. "We knew we were looking at something wonderful," said Steve Squyres, director of scientific operations. At first, no one was sure what the unusual rock showed. Later, everyone agreed that this rock, nicknamed "El Capitan," was proof that the place the rock came from had once been a large, <u>shallow</u> sea. If life ever developed on Mars, it would most likely happen in a shallow sea.

<u>shallow</u>: not deep

Mission Accomplished

A rover's life span depends on the energy its solar panels and batteries make. When a lot of dust falls on the solar panels, they stop working. The batteries do not recharge endlessly. When it is winter on Mars, the days become shorter. The sun is lower in the sky. The solar panels cannot produce a lot of energy, so the mission ends.

Scientists originally predicted that each rover would last for 90 sols. However, both rovers worked for more than 150 days. They worked almost three times longer than the scientists had hoped.

Sojourner studied the ➲ rocks on Mars for clues to the planet's history.

↻ The layers and wrinkles in this rock show that it was made as sediments drifted down through water over a long time.

Chapter Four

The Future on Mars

The President of the United States recently set a goal for the next space mission. The mission is to send people to Mars. This is a huge mission! More than three hundred people worked to put two rovers on Mars. It will take many, many more workers to send people there.

Mars: Just Another Moon Mission?

Humans have already walked on the moon several times. However, there are some important differences between a mission to the moon and a mission to Mars. One important difference is that the Moon is much closer to Earth than Mars.

People often call Mars the Red ⮑
Planet because it looks red from
Earth. Mars actually has many colors.

It took astronauts four days to get to the moon in 1969. It will take astronauts over seven months to get to Mars. Because it takes so long to get to Mars, astronauts would stay there longer, too. A round-trip mission to Mars could last about three years.

NASA is developing ways that people can be in space for three years. Scientists need to find a way for people to make their own food, water, and oxygen. Some people have practiced missions to Mars in places that are similar to Mars, like Antarctica.

However, we need to learn more about Mars before people can go there safely. For example, we know there is more deadly solar **radiation** on Mars than on Earth. Also, dust on Mars may have higher levels of **toxic** metals. People will not go to Mars until many, many years from now!

Conclusion

Over the past 30 years we have learned some amazing things about Mars. From the information that *Spirit* and *Opportunity* collected, we now know Mars once had oceans. It is exciting to think about the possibility that these oceans had living things. Steve Squyres reminds us to remember the most amazing thing about the Mars missions. The missions are all great works of engineering, the designing and building of machines. He says: "It's funny. When we first built [*Spirit* and *Opportunity*], we babied them. Now they're scratched, beat up, and dirty. We have pushed them to their limits on Mars. . . . And they, by being so capable, are pushing us to our limits as we find new things for them to do."

Glossary

bacteria a one-celled organism *(page 5)*

gravity the force that pulls us toward the ground *(page 4)*

lander the part of the spacecraft that lands on Mars *(page 3)*

Martian a creature or thing from Mars *(page 5)*

mission a trip by a spacecraft into space *(page 2)*

navigation moving around in a directed way *(page 10)*

orbiter an instrument that circles a planet and sends back information *(page 6)*

probe any instrument that makes contact with another planet or moon and sends back information *(page 6)*

radiation waves sent out by the Sun. Strong radiation can be dangerous *(page 20)*

rover a small vehicle that moves around on a planet or moon and sends back information *(page 2)*

satellite a spacecraft that can orbit, or circle around, a planet *(page 6)*

sol a Martian day *(page 14)*

solar system the nine planets that orbit the sun *(page 5)*

toxic poisonous *(page 20)*

Index

bacteria, *5*

gravity, *4*

Jet Propulsion Laboratory, *2*

lander, *3, 11–13*

Martian, *5, 20*

mission, *2, 6, 7, 9, 17, 18, 20, 21*

moon, *18–20*

NASA, *9, 11, 20*

navigation, *10, 12–14*

Opportunity, 9, 11, 14, 16, 21

orbiter, *6, 7*

probe, *6, 7*

radiation, *20*

rover, *2, 7–17, 18, 21*

satellite, *6, 7*

Sojourner, 7, 8, 10, 17

sol, *14, 17*

solar system, *1*

Spirit, 2, 3, 9, 11, 14, 16, 21

Squyres, Steven, *16, 21*

Theisinger, Paul, *9–10*

Viking, 6, 7

water, *5, 8, 9, 16–17, 21*

Comprehension Check

Summarize

Complete the Summary Chart with the class. Summarize the story. You can use the chart to help you organize your ideas.

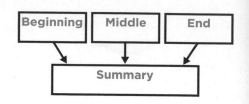

Think and Compare

1. Look at page 12. What do scientists do while the rovers are traveling to Mars? *(Summarize)*

2. What are some of the things you do when you plan a project to build something? *(Analyze)*

3. Should we send people to live and work on Mars? Why or why not? *(Evaluate)*